THE

CANDLELIT

HOME

THE CANDLELIT HOME

Decorating with Candles Year-Round

John Terrell Fry

Photographs by Nancy Nolan

HARRY N. ABRAMS, PUBLISHERS, INC.

EDITOR: Ellen Nidy
DESIGNER: Dana Sloan

Library of Congress Control Number: 2001089396
ISBN 0–8109–0608–2 (Abrams) — 0–8109–1148–5 (Homes for Living)

Printed and bound in Hong Kong

10 9 8 7 6 5 4 3

Harry N. Abrams, Inc.
100 Fifth Avenue
New York, N.Y. 10011
www.abramsbooks.com

To my mother, Erdine

To Michael Laughter for The Story of Light and the

brilliant captions that helped me set the tone and capture

the spirit of this book.

I would especially like to thank the people without whom this book

would not have been possible: Thom Hall; Rus Venable; Stephen

Lanford; Brett Pitts; Kevin Walsh; Ellen Scruggs.

IMPORTANT TIPS FOR BURNING CANDLES RESPONSIBLY

A few simple measures will insure your safety while you enjoy your candlelit home. Burn your candles mindfully. Always place candles in or on proper nonflammable candle holders, well away from any flammable material. Direct drafts can cause uneven burning. Keep lit candles out of the reach of children and pets. Trim the wick to $\frac{1}{4}$ inch before lighting or relighting. Remove any foreign objects, such as matches and wick trimmings, from the wax pool. Allow candles to cool before relighting. Never move a lit candle, as the melted wax may spill. To extinguish candles use a snuffer, or cup your hand an inch or two behind the flame and blow gently. To remove candles from decorative, reusable candle holders, put the holders in the freezer for a short time, which will cause the wax to contract and pop out.

Most important, always be sure to extinguish all candles before going to bed. NEVER leave burning candles unattended.

CONTENTS

The flowers are arranged, the silver is polished, and everything is in order. The guests will arrive any minute. You light the candles and admire their magic. With the first flicker of light you are inspired by memories of other special occasions by candlelight.

We all begin with one simple candle. Then, birthday by birthday, we light one after another, creating an ever-expanding reach of light. When you think about it, you realize every celebration is enhanced by candlelight.

My favorite use of candles is with flowers. Light and nature together create a magical environment that we want to share with people who are important to us. By creating an ambience with light and fragrance, we are letting people know we care about them. Our homes are made more beautiful when illuminated by candlelight, and our friends are more welcomed by our use of it. Whether it's a single votive or a vast bank of columns, candles enhance any celebration and allow us to emphasize the importance of the moment.

Vanilla votive candles nested in coffee beans atop an Italian footed bowl set the tone for a light breakfast. As the candles warm up the coffee beans, they release a rich aroma that reinforces the promise of a cup to come.

10

My interest in flowers and gardening started with my grandmother. She directed the garden while my grandfather and I toiled in the trenches. From the first sprout poking through the soil to the harvest, I became hooked. As a minister's wife, my grandmother was a devoted entertainer of the community. It was a task she relished and she recruited her grandchildren to help her on it. It seemed that almost every week someone was celebrating a birthday in her home. When the cake was baked and the candles were carefully placed on it, I was often the honored one who, armed with scissors, would harvest that week's zinnias, roses, or whatever was blooming in the garden. A partnership of flowers and candles was quickly formed in my mind, and I can no longer imagine one without the other.

I took a job in a flower shop while I was still in school, and for the next six years I worked as a floral designer for Tipton & Hurst in Little Rock, Arkansas. I went on to teach floral design at the University of Arkansas and conduct seminars throughout the United States, and was ultimately inducted into the American Institute of Floral Design.

I was soon designing and developing products for the floral and gift trade. I traveled often on business, and my dream of seeing the world came one step closer to being realized when China opened its doors to international trade in the 1980s. After attending a gift fair there, I traveled throughout the country touring factories, which gave me a glimpse of a culture that had been sheltered from Western influences. I ate simple meals in simple settings, by candlelight with fresh peonies. I collected many of the beautiful things that I found and carried around two heavy stone fu dogs and a large satchel full of ox-blood vases, knowing the inconvenience was worth it.

This trip whetted my appetite for travel and collecting, and three continents and twelve countries later, my basement is full. However, these trips are not the only reason for the clutter under my house. I have a lifelong hobby of searching through yard sales and flea markets, even while close to home. The treasures I collect, whether from near or far, have always influenced and inspired my designs.

When I started my home fragrance company, Seasons, I kept my day job and worked evenings and weekends on my new product line. I would leave the hot warehouse reeking of the fragrances we were creating and covered with dye the shade of the raffia we were using to close the bags of potpourri. The process was not glamorous; it was just plain messy, but very rewarding.

With the success of Seasons I began looking to purchase my first home. I found one that was charming but needed a great deal of restoration, which yielded its own surprises and opportunities. While clearing the underbrush from the backyard, I was thrilled to find, unexpectedly, the remnants of an English garden—here was ther perfect place to continue my love of growing roses. When I had finally completed the remodeling, I was left with a great, but empty, home. An art dealer approached me, asking to showcase her collections in the house. During the next six art shows, I fell in love with every piece, and purchased my favorites. This delayed furniture buying for a few more years as I concentrated on collecting art. Every morning I was content to have a cup of coffee in my new art gallery home. My love of my house and my art has grown throughout my career, and living and entertaining with an ever-changing art collection has taught me to look at the simple elements of candles and flowers in a more focused way.

While working on a Seasons' catalogue shoot, I met the photographer Stephen Landford. Impressed with his expertise, I shared with him my aspirations of creating a book about candles as a decorative element. He suggested I meet his wife, Nancy Nolan. I'm sure it sounded like a project he was dumping on her, and consequently we didn't meet right away. Quite by accident, months later,

Nancy and I worked together photographing the Seasons' product introductions. As she was lighting the first set, I realized I had not only found a partner for my book, but a new best friend. My friendship with Nancy and her family has been a great joy. Her work is impeccable and incredibly sensitive.

Throughout this book we have suggested different ways of using color, texture, light, and collectibles to create an environment. Many of the objects we used were incorporated from the endless supply of finds in my basement, as well as my friends' basements. It was important to me that we use fresh flowers, real fruit, and no artificial or dried materials. It is apparent from the photographs that I have no intention of hiding the flaws of the blossoms and fruit. My favorite aspect of nature is its beautiful delicacy and fleeting splendor.

As I was scouting locations for the book, I realized I didn't have to go any farther than my own community— all of the photographs were taken in Little Rock, Arkansas. When you open your eyes to look at what is around you, you often discover great materials and settings within arm's reach. With a little creativity, you can transform your home and everyday objects into a beautiful backdrop. Candles are an integral part of this transformation—you can create the perfect setting for a birthday, an anniversary, or an intimate personal moment by using candles.

Creating this book has been a dream of mine for many years. I have long recited the definition of "creative" to my associates. A creative person is one who *does* something. It's that simple. I hope this compilation of our work inspires you to create, or to do, what you dream.

—JOHN TERRELL FRY

The Story of Light

The first human endeavor to harness the elements resulted in portable fire. Magical in its purity, the candle embodies earth, wind, and the last brilliant element. Light never leaves the modern world. We throw a switch, wave our hands, twist a knob, even clap, and banish the dark. Our lighting consists of lumens, incandescence, tungsten filaments, watts, mercury fluorescence, and halogen. It rarely occurs to us that until recently, candles were our sole allies against shadows. Accompanied by their glow we plotted intrigues, wrote or obscured history, dreamed myths, agonized over or celebrated love, planned campaigns, scrawled sonnets, authored manuscripts.

Books and newspapers may have been printed, but until the mid-nineteenth century, the rolling presses were illuminated by candlelight. Humans might find comfort in the light of day, but we have lived and recorded our lives in the glow of candles. Sounds romantic, doesn't it? The purpose of this book is to illustrate how to inject a little bit of that romance back into our harried lives. We aren't suggesting candles to provide mere task lighting: They can provide contrasts, meld shadows, and enhance any area in which we live.

The origins of portable light, while lost in the mists of history, certainly marked the progress of civilization. The earliest forms of lamps were shells or horns filled

with animal fat, and a green twig or plant fiber for a wick. Mediterranean cultures pressed olives and pooled the oil into intricately carved vessels, creating a steady, if smoky, light. Indian temple lights were formulated from wax skimmed off boiling cinnamon. In pre-Columbian America, tribes used an oily fish wedge in the fork of a stick. (Imagine the smell within the lodge or hut!) Any available resource would be used to sustain light.

The word "candle" is thought to derive from the Latin *candela*, a further derivation of *candere*, to burn, or possibly from the early Danish *kindil*, meaning to burn or kindle. *Taper*, originally a very thin candle made before the advent of candle molds in the fifteenth century, comes from Old or Middle English.

Rush lights, created from cattails or swordlike grasses dipped in fat, provided further smoky illumination until medieval times, when chandlers traversed the countryside creating tapers from tallow or beeswax for individual households. Glass lanterns, to prevent guttering and extinguished candles, appear after the fall of the Roman Empire when the windows of kings' and warlords' great drafty halls were open to the elements. Expensive and difficult to produce, glass was far too precious to use for windows.

Tallow, the vital candle ingredient, was rendered fat, and had a distinct odor. Neighbors complained when candle factories opened on their streets, creating a stench. Even snuffing out the tallow candle did not eradicate its smell. Melted tallow from candles was used to waterproof boots, and when people had head colds, they "tallowed" their noses to keep them from running (let's hope they couldn't smell it). You knew you had made it into the middle class when you were able to burn the sweeter beeswax. In addition, beeswax burns at a slightly

lower temperature, making the flame paler, and almost white, instead of the distinct gold cast by tallow. Even if visitors could not smell your relative affluence, they knew it from the light given off by your candles. By 1850, it was said that only an Eskimo—meaning only an individual far, far from civilization—would burn tallow candles. Later, stearic acid combined with paraffin made candles more resistant to temperature changes and enabled them to burn longer. Bayberry was used in New England to create a scented product but then, as now, it was almost prohibitive in cost: it takes almost two quarts of the wax from the tiny berries to produce a regular taper.

Gas replaced candlelight, electricity replaced gas; both sources cheap and bountiful, yet we cling to our candles. They ornament our first birthday cake, they glow upon altars at our wedding. Available in many sizes, shapes, and colors, they provide shimmer and ambience in our lives, Scented, they add yet another

dimension. Chandlers of old would be amazed at their proliferation. We aren't advocating a return to the days when candlelight was all we had to extend our lives past twilight, but we know candles can provide warmth, welcome, and perspective. King Ludwig of Bavaria, in his worship of Louis XIV and everything the Sun King built, produced an exact copy of the Hall of Mirrors at Versailles, where he proceeded to burn 4,000 candles every night. Few of us can erect such a shrine now—just think of the numbers of people necessary to light all those candles— but we can use a single votive, or drifts of them, to define a walk, highlight a mantel or table, provide romance where there might otherwise be none. Prometheus stole fire from heaven so mankind could do more than subsist on this earth. We can use it to make our lives more interesting, and yes, more romantic. We continue to hold back the night.

—MICHAEL LAUGHTER

The indulgence of candlelight in a spring garden is magical and within our reach. Spring always surprises and delights me. It generates an abundant supply of foliage and flowers as well as a change in light and color. What a perfect time to introduce the use of candlelight to extend the lavish displays of spring. As I watch the days grow longer, new beginnings surround me. Gardens burst with a thousand shades of green that lift our spirits and seem to offer permission to play with color. Pinks and whites enter the landscape next and team with new greens to create a balanced color scheme. Suddenly there is an explosion of bright yellows as the daffodils march across the garden and the forsythia waves back. Magnificent shades of every hue invigorate our spirits. Feelings of euphoria unfold with each sign of new life.

OPPOSITE: When you have an artifact in your garden, make use of it. We centered the setting for our spring wedding around a time-etched statue. We selected bowl-shaped candles, which create their own chimney as they burn. The tall candle holders also contain a vase for flowers. We covered the tables with a peach cloth, stapled inexpensive tulle for full skirts all around, and circled them with boxwood. We tied the remnants of the tulle around the chair backs. With the twinkle of the candles, and the sparkle of conversation, your tables become a corps de ballet for the journey of afternoon into evening.

We chose antique Wedgwood majolica for its deep malachite color. The color of foliage "settles" any setting. As the petals drift downward, leave them where they drop, in the hurricane laterns, on the tablecloth, or on plates.

This season offers an opportunity to bring the outside in and carry the inside out. Candles contribute to the growth of romance, which plays a leading role at this time of year. You may suspend the darkness with the soft flicker of candles, or you may use them to complement night's natural beauty.

When I look out of my living room window into the garden, I'm inspired to have a candlelit gathering. The ancient tulip tree is the first to show its new colors. Like most spring-blossoming trees in the South, the display is glorious but short. To take advantage of its bouquet and the ever-changing color, I hang lanterns on the lower branches, attaching them with ribbons of varying lengths. The suspended candles allowed my guests and me to view the spectacular display well into the evening. The light added stars to the garden and made the view more alluring from the living room windows.

The glow of the lanterns seemed to pull everyone outside. For once guests gathered in the intimate settings of the yard rather than in the brightly lit kitchen. We all struggle with kitchen-bound visitors—the success of a gathering might well be determined by the headcount in your kitchen. It is nice to take advantage of all the room you have, indoors and out, to make the evening go smoothly.

Prolong an enchanted evening in a blooming garden seated at a table laden with candles. Create your own fairy tale as the garden awakens. Giant azaleas and ancient tulip trees provide a great centerpiece, but the results can be just as beautiful in your own backyard. Bring out your favorite candle holders, hurricanes for the table, and garden stakes to light the paths. Position the containers to create pools of candlelight. For extra accent, as well as light, add hanging lanterns from a favorite tree or attach them to a garden wall.

OPPOSITE: Is there anything better than a spring evening? Why sit inside and view it through a window? We hung lanterns on ribbon that matched the pink blossoms of the ancient Japanese magnolia outside the living room windows. Two somewhat stiff salon chairs were recruited for irony, a card table was draped with bark cloth, and oversize hurricanes purchased from a Mexican artifacts store provide lighting at eye level. Serve a light repast on porcelain and use cutlery meant for the dining table. Then throw open the windows so you can hear the Liszt études or jazz waft out into the spring air.

With columns formed by a pair of river birch trees and walls of draping white azaleas, our out-door buffet sits perfectly in a room formed by nature. The candles and crystal blend together, enhancing the natural lighting of the evening.

Create your own candle containers from something as simple as a lemon. First, we cut off about a third of the "top" portion (the "bottom" is the stem end, which provides a more even base), and then we hulled the lemon using a sharp knife. A candle fits snugly inside, and as it burns, the rind emits a pleasant citrus smell. We place a few of our lemon votives in a bowl containing whole lemons and ivy leaves.

OVERLEAF: Yellow flowers on our sideboard create their own glow for evening. The little blue votives have the feel of luminaria.

OPPOSITE: Use your collections. We wanted clean lines and we limited our colors, so we selected contemporary silver candle holders, a sterling top-hat cigarette holder, and Italian cobalt. We wanted sheen and glimmer, but only had white tapers on hand, so we sprayed them yellow with florist paint to stay within our palette.

Candles raise our spirits when spring rains and cool evenings cause a retreat back inside. Gather a handful of daffodils and tulips, search the cupboards for old cobalt, silver candlesticks, and glass containers, and celebrate the arrival of spring inside, within the realm of candlelight. The bottomless blue of cobalt glass has always been irresistible to me. A Carlo Noretti bowl resting in a silver cradle is a perfect example. This bowl started my cobalt collection, which keeps growing. Daffodils, tulips, and lemons seem especially happy in each other's company. Tall candles the color of the flowers draw you into the tablescape. Using opposing colors, like blue and yellow, gives this arrangement a vivid charm that might not be achieved with another color of candle. Nothing brings out the happiness of yellow like deep, bottomless cobalt blue. Since I had only white candles, I sprayed them with florist paint. You don't have to be limited to a simple glass votive cup. Cutting a lemon in half and making a cavity for the candle is an easy way to create a votive holder.

Candles have broken free of their traditional molds. The variety of candles available in the marketplace extends beyond the imagination. Artisans around the world have created all types of shapes and finishes in thousands of colors. One of the candles I use weighs thirty pounds. Others simulate blossoms and are so delicate that the artist's fingerprints show through the thin layers of wax making up the petals. Wax is always ready to take a colorist at his word. Most of the time I enjoy traditional round column candles in neutral palates because they are the most versatile. However, there are other times when you can add charm, beauty, or an element of surprise with a candle that is artfully crafted.

OPPOSITE: A tablescape of a tag-sale urn with crape myrtle, and past-their-prime hydrangeas from the garden. RIGHT: A delicate wax rose with a votive nestled inside.

Flowers on fire—mix the real with the imagined. Classic forms and materials, such as roses, translate well into other mediums. Here, wax roses blend in a nosegay with their counterparts.

Floating candles are a charming way to create a focal point. I go to the garden, pick a few blooms, purchase some floating candles, and drop them all in a crystal bowl. The type of crystal bowl may vary. Use the container of your choice, anything from a wine glass to a punch bowl. For a more casual look you might use mason jars and zinnias. Floating candles vary, as well. The flowerlike candles I used were from the "sale" table at a craft store. Their simple design allowed the pansy "faces" to take the spotlight.

Floating flames and flowers—go to the garden, pick a few blooms, purchase some floating candles, and drop them all in a crystal bowl. It's effortless and you have three of the elements: earth, water, and fire.

37

OPPOSITE: Pale pink pillars, turned into art objects, rest on a crystal cake stand, which has a lip, so we were able to float dahlias and cyclamen foliage in water.

With a little imagination you can turn an ordinary candle into your personal work of art. While waiting to pay for my latest finds at an estate sale, I heard a lady say, "I wish there were two of these." She was looking through a box of mismatched jewelry. This box of shiny, disregarded, costume pieces instantly caught my attention. Five dollars later, I had a fistful of loot that I took back to my nest. Mother's Day was approaching, and I had an idea. My mother's favorite color is pink, so I started with pale pink column candles. I retrieved the box of ribbon and cording from the attic and selected a fuchsia silk cord. After wrapping the candles in the cording, I simply clipped on the earrings and pinned on the brooches. My Mother's Day gift of candles was dressed for the occasion, the perfect complement to a beautiful bouquet of garden flowers.

Jeweled flames—what about all those solitary mismatched earrings you find at tag sales? We took a handful and clipped them to ribbons wound around column candles.

38

BELOW, RIGHT AND OPPOSITE:
A solitary votive candle, surrounded by hellebore and
hydrangea, rests on a sterling
Victorian dog bowl. Hellebore,
so delicate in candlelight, is
among the first garden blooms.

BELOW, LEFT: All dressed up and
ready to burn—is your candle
not the right shade? Wrap it in
ribbon. Fabric provides texture
and color for your flame. We
tied a bow, inserted a cyclamen
bud and leaf, and set our man-
nequin in a small silver compote. We partnered it with a
votive in a blown rose perched
in an antique silver salt dish.

Since I have designed candles for years, I have
kept many candles that aren't really perfect. Actually, I
have a large collection of candles that other people
would have thrown out. Meanwhile, I spot a spool of
lavender millinery ribbon that screams out to be used.
Searching through the leftover candles I find one that's
discolored, but otherwise very usable. The ribbon wrap
gives it a color and texture, making it a candidate for a
place of prominence. Positioned atop a silver urn, this
candle finds a new home.

40

We've taken a winter-tarnished yard
ornament, a miniature bird bath,
adorned it with white smilax berries,
a votive, and added our own clutch
of quail eggs to echo the mottled
birds and to remind us of spring.

Candles can turn a beautiful setting into a breath-taking vision. A longtime friend invited me to visit his garden, so I drove downtown to his home in the historic Quapaw district in Little Rock. As I entered Thom's antique brick pathway, masses of white azaleas surrounded us, creating entire rooms complete with ceilings. Even the ground was carpeted white with petals. We were presented with the perfect site for hosting a garden buffet. Using candles, high and low, gave the illusion of fireflies glimmering from blossom to blossom. By candlelight, the crystal champagne flutes, crisp white linens, and pale blush azaleas turned to gold as the evening progressed. As I looked at the candlelit tables, a certain quality of light, color, and texture made me think of beautiful damask. Breaking away from the traditional pair of candlesticks, I used a combination of low candles to put light onto the tabletops. In an intimate setting such as this, candlesticks would place the flame at eye level, making conversation difficult. The crystal rose bowls protect the flame, cast the glow from the tabletop, and refract the light while creating an elegance with simple garden-themed candle stands.

OPPOSITE: Azaleas in Thom's backyard

Masses of white flowers, a table for two nestled on a brick path, a bowl of azaleas, and simple votives and torchieres light up the afternoon, or hold back the night.

Inside the house we continued the theme and used white for everything. White candles in garden ornaments, white cauliflower cored for votives, and white roses at each place setting. The cauliflower was also used as a vase for the roses. Sheer white linens and white mesh luminaria gave the simple table an elegant feel that reflects the garden's intimate setting. I took a winter-tarnished yard ornament—a miniature birdbath—and added white smilax berries, a votive, and a clutch of quail eggs to echo the mottled effect of the birds (see pp. 42–43). The use of outdoor accessories such as bird eggs and luminary bags draws us back to the garden just as the crystal rose bowls did. Frosted votive cups and martini glasses play up the white idea. This enchanted evening will become a yearly tradition.

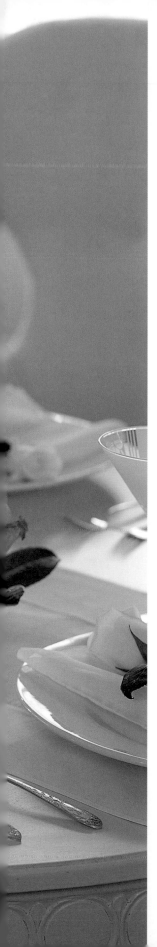

After a long winter, spring evenings
have real enchantment. Layers of
light and white—an uncomplicated
table setting incorporating simple
votives and perfect roses nestled in
cauliflower with luminaria and gos-
samer linen.

Whether using candles in the living room or in the garden, their glow enhances the beautiful bounty of spring. Extending your home to include the outdoors is an important bonus of this season, especially after being trapped indoors during the winter months. I am content to work in my garden as long as the light will allow. At the end of the day I light the candles on the patio, in the garden, and at the gate to invite others to enjoy the spectacle—but I must admit, I do it for myself as much as for others. I tend to plant things that bloom all season. Cutting flowers for the house is my way of bringing the season inside. Flowers and candles are the perfect combination—I enjoy them best together, celebrating the rites of spring by candlelight.

By candlelight the crystal champagne flutes, votive-filled rose bowls, and crisp white linens turn golden as the evening progresses. The clusters of grapes seem gilded. The silver pieces echo the amber tones.

Summer roses are one of my favorite things about the season. My love of them together with candlelight began when I was a child. Growing up, all the elements of summer weather seemed to work against the cables of electricity that swagged their way to our farm in Hope, Arkansas. Power lines were often knocked down by storms. This meant we were accustomed to candles as a source of light. As to my fondness for roses, I inherited that from my father. According to his philosophy, roses were grown for the soul; all other crops supported the farm. When I was ten my father and I planted a rose garden. As soon as the first blossoms appeared, I was hooked on flowers and gardening. Our lifestyle was simple, but we always had summer roses and, out of necessity, candles, too. All these years later, I'm still growing roses, and candles are just as important to me, with or without electricity.

THE BOUNTY OF SUMMER

Golden, travertine-finished candles
echo the marble finish of the urn
and accent the array of jewel-toned
flowers, drawing the eye upward
to the pineapple—the universal
symbol of hospitality.

An early Saturday morning trip to our local
farmer's market brings back memories of the family
farm. Summer brings us a wonderful crop of locally
grown produce. Fresh flowers, fruit, and vegetables are a
great way to begin arrangements for entertaining.

A candlelit pineapple's hospitality is a perfect way to
welcome guests with the bounty of summer. Since summer is one of the easiest times to entertain, I like to be as
welcoming as possible. Big outdoor entertaining was the
best part of this season when I was growing up—and,
actually, that hasn't changed. What has changed is that
now I have the responsibility for making the guests
feel at home. Whether using contrasting candle colors
or a repeating color theme, candles can help establish
the mood for any kind of gathering you would like.
Travertine-finished candles growing out of marble urns
are a beautiful contrast with a colorful floral bouquet.

The chartreuse candles I found were perfect with Mint Julep roses. When I added them to the collection of green grapes, limes, honeydew melon, and a blown-glass pineapple, they almost cooled down the room. Gathering different shades of the same color in the accessories makes a foyer table more noticeable. Contrast is the key. Whether matte, shiny, pale, or dark I used all the green I had on hand. Then, for punch, I used the opposite color, violet statice, which makes the green stand out. The effect is refreshing.

57

MIXED GREENS

Only with light can there be color. And is there a cooler, more satisfying color than green? Matte and shiny, pale and dark, we used all the ranges of green we had at hand. What's so wonderful here is that you can eat almost everything when you are through. The satin-glass pineapple light is from a tag sale, as is the footed compote. We stuffed violet statice into the McCoy bowl to contrast with the green. By the way, the roses are called "Mint Julep." Doesn't that quench your thirst?

Illuminate a treasure. In this instance, it's a scrap of eccentrically monogrammed silk found at a jumble sale. The silver dishes, filled with arrangements, are crowned with votive candles. The flickering candles play up the sheen of the fabric, continuing the glow of a summer day.

Sometimes neutral-colored candles work best. If you are trying to show off a strong collection of accessories or a special new addition, simple, natural colors are essential. I used carnations in treasured silver urns illuminated with simple votives. The tapestry that the urns are resting on is, of course, an estate-sale find. The colors of the tapestry are highlighted by the colors of the carnations. The neutral color of the candles ensures that the flowers, fabric, and compotes get the attention they deserve.

White and ivory candles are as classic as a string of pearls. I feel the same is true for blue-and-white porcelain. It goes with everything from Levis to linen. Through the years I have collected enough to do a state dinner, and summer is the perfect time to use these crisp, cool colors. To keep things light and breezy, I let daisies have room to sway in the center of the table. In this case, I decided it was all right to risk having the dinner conversation slightly impaired by a daisy or two. Cobalt votive cups filled with white candles repeat the patterns on the dinnerware. Underneath it all is a vintage blue-and-white tablecloth that was folded for so many years that no amount of ironing will take out the creases. Getting carried away, I decided that it might be fun to include the dining chairs in the color scheme. Since I was not expecting overnight guests, I jerked the white matelassé coverlets from the twin guest beds and used them as slipcovers. I secured the covers to the chairs with some leftover "it's a boy" blue ribbon. At the top of each chair back I pinned a smart bow and inserted a single daisy. The candlelight reflecting on the sleek blue wine glasses gave the setting a fantasy feeling.

Is there anything so fresh and uncomplicated as blue and white? We mixed Japanese, Dutch, and English export china—Blue Onion, Blue Willow, and other patterns —an antique tablecloth, and wildflowers in a tureen topped with a small candle, then sprinkled blue votives around the table.

Outdoor entertaining is more relaxed, but it still has all the possibilities of indoor parties. An outdoor chandelier brings the same air of formality to an intimate garden setting as its indoor counterpart. As the candles burn, the wax drips and adds to the drama of this unusual garden accessory. Suspended from a high bough, it seems to be from another place and time. For larger gatherings, I scatter dining tables on the porch and let them spill into the garden. At Robert's party we dressed the tables with formal damask cloths. Then we created perimeters of each dining area with glowing candles that hugged the large tables, making each more intimate. The evening sky is lifted by lamps that were designed to hold two or more candles. Candles beckoning guests from the garden gate to the front porch will cause neighbors and passers-by to wish they were invited to this party. A path of luminaria leading to candlelit tables relaxes and charms away the activities of the day.

For divine decadence, hang a chandelier from a tree limb. Allow the candles to burn and drowse until the wax drips.

One of summer's drawbacks is the void left by the now unnecessary fireplace. As I walk through Nancy's house on a really humid July afternoon, we both comment on its emptiness. We were planning a wedding reception for the following weekend, and the bride established the color theme of whites and off-whites. Candles will be our primary source of light. We want the guests to be able to celebrate the occasion in a relaxed and glowing atmosphere. To make use of the fireplace, I found a large pewter tray to place on the floor and reflect the glow. Then, using candles leftover from previous parties, we arranged them with the tallest in the back. We used all sizes to create random heights and plays of light. Candles were repeated on the mantel. We used pewter goblets to hold column candles.

What to do with a fireplace in the summertime? Logs piled inside in August look absurd; greenery placed there can appear as if you forgot to take your pruned foliage to the curb; left empty, fireplaces can look like gaping mouths without teeth. We gathered up all the column candles in the house, placed them on a pewter tray to reflect the glow, and arranged the tallest ones at the back. All your candles of different ages and sizes can be used—you don't want uniformity, or even the same color. Candles placed on the mantel, as well as within the fireplace, balance the room.

BELOW, LEFT: A classic urn *à la* Carmen Miranda. Take a charger broad enough to close the opening, fill it with various sizes and heights of pillar candles, and trim with greenery, flowers, and ribbon.

BELOW, RIGHT: The smallest effects are the sweetest. A column candle placed into a sweetmeat dish and trimmed with arrangement leftovers creates a glow in an otherwise forgotten corner of the room.

In keeping with the color theme, we decorated with ivory ribbons and white flowers. Garden urns topped with candles on a charger were placed in front of the windows to balance the light in the room. Candles incorporated in unexpected places add interest to different corners of the rooms. A small votive next to a stack of books makes the titles mysterious. Silver cups holding candles placed next to flowers and collectibles create still-life vignettes throughout the home. At this summer wedding, the central fireplace maintained its status as the welcoming focus of the room.

OPPOSITE: Outdoor textures are never uniform, so we choose a silk-glass candle lamp for height, a mottled column candle, flickering votives, and a soft cantalope-hued damask cloth. All plays well within the generous recesses of the front porch.

Since the heart of the room is the dining table, I like to reinforce the importance of the tablescape by starting with a theme. Themes can be as simple or as contrived as you like. For Holly's dinner party, I chose to keep it tropical but elegant. We selected Hermès' newest place settings and foliage-green embroidered tablecloth of fine polished cotton. Random miniature candles highlighted exotic orchids. The feeling of a cool tropical evening encased the room.

ABOVE: Use a teacup to transplant an orchid at each place setting. It's unexpectedly elegant and it lowers the blossoms to the height of the votives.

Unexpected components create
visual interest. We started with
topiary forms, and placed
column candles on top and
mixed arrangements below.
We used the table from the
potting shed, floral patterned
china, real linen, silver, and
crystal, and brought out the
kitchen chairs. And we placed
it all poolside.

75

A gateway of light draws in your guests. We wanted luminaria, but instead of the sand-weighted bags we found these Mexican glass jars. We enhanced the structure of the garden wall with the uniform placement of our candles. The towers are garden pieces, but instead of potted plants we used candles and mixed flowers on the shelves.

Undulating candle flames provide a living frame for our guests.

In contrast, the next setting uses a repeating theme to frame a refreshing, afternoon tea. Raspberry is the flavor of the day. Attention to detail is important in this theme. I chose candles, blossoms, and even cookies that repeated the raspberry notion. The tea itself, in a sleek crystal pitcher, reflects the candles and duplicates the colors of the roses, lilies, and hydrangeas. A tall bronze candelabrum lifts the centerpiece of flowers and candles overhead, creating a canopy. Candles are used not only to light the table, but to lightly scent the room with the fresh aroma of raspberries.

We began with raspberry iced tea and finished with raspberry compote. We never tired of the color or taste. Take one color and play with it, sustain it, and keep your surroundings light. Individual candles, embroidered linens, and sumptuous summer flowers make for a heady experience.

We lit the steps leading us into the secret garden, where candles winked at us, as inviting as fireflies. Juxtaposing fire and water, we used votives on mirrors to reflect and refract the light. To create your own water shrine, take a simple mirror and attach it to a wreath form of styrofoam with florist's clay. Then escape to your own fantasy island.

The heat of summer draws us to the cooling comfort of water. Sanderson's beautiful water garden is a great example of the simple tranquility that water and candlelight can create. Steps leading down to the garden were lit with a collection of votive cups and lanterns. The pool was filled with aquatic plants and highlighted with floating platforms of candles. We created these reflective islands by attaching round mirrors to styrofoam wreath forms. Water on the mirrors picks up the candles' light and refracts it as the currents move.

Another way to enjoy the element of water is to create a spa in your own bath. Whether you have a claw-foot tub, a jacuzzi, or simply a shower stall, you can add a new dimension to bath time. A drift of votives, some lined with cucumber slices for a hint of a refreshing fragrance, or a few column candles at different heights, help transform ablution into a solution for tension. I used sunflowers because their brilliant gold petals hold the light and mirror the glow of the flame. Add your favorite bath salts and settle in. Summer should be a time of reflection and relaxation, but that's not always easy to squeeze into our schedules. Enjoying water by candlelight is an opportunity to treat yourself to a break from summer's heat.

Add another dimension to bath time with layers of light and sunflowers.

84

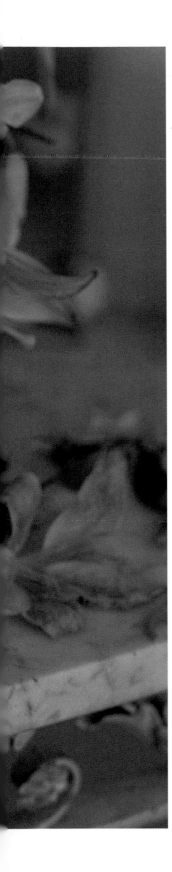

However you spend your summer, indoors or out, entertaining or relaxing, candles help to highlight your activities. Accenting the collections we have, or filling the voids of fireplaces we can't use, candles focus our attention on the moment. Their light guides our guests and completes our atmosphere. Adding the calming element of water provides us with the retreat we need from bright lights and computer screens. Although I am reluctant to give up the last bouquet of summer, doing so gives me an opportunity to create the ideal tribute—nesting a votive in the remains of a shattered blossom is a beautiful way to sustain the last rose of the season.

Did you ever want to extend the life of a flower? We took from the garden two full-blown, pale pink roses about to shatter, carefully removed the stems, peeled a strip of petals from one, settled it on the table, and placed a votive candle in the flower. We set the second rose in the wrought-iron votive stand, placing the candle directly in it. Don't discard the petals you remove—scatter them on the table, and set your candles on them. Remember, a small display of candles can be as effective as an entire roomful, and the materials you have on hand add texture.

Autumn's dramatic display of vivid colors is like art on the canvas of the trees and shrubs surrounding us. The beauty of this season causes me to stop and study the work of nature. My own art collection began with Andy Warhol's lithograph of *The Witch*. It perfectly illustrates my love of this time of year. This character of the witch from *The Wizard of Oz* has been a dominating force in my house year round and has caused me to look at fall in a different way. But even though I pass a witch as I go to bed every night, the ghosts and ghouls of Halloween are not what I love the most. The child in me has never grown out of looking forward to this magical season when the lush summer foliage I so enjoyed has changed to the colorful displays of the harvest. The leaf-covered path to my home is reminiscent of the yellow brick road in *The Wizard of Oz*.

RUSTIC GLOW

Fall is a golden time. Extend it with the simple glow of a votive in a crackle-glass cup. The grapes on the tablecloth echo the shape and the gold of the flame.

OPPOSITE: We include all the colors of autumn leaves without picking a single one. Mix your linens and flowers, and by all means use variations of candle shapes and colors.

When cool evenings bring you back into the comfort of your living room, you might use large candles to mimic the outdoors. Candles come in myriad shapes, and I found one that was molded from a concrete garden urn. Perched on an antique French pedestal, this dramatic candle invites guests to view the garden from the small iron balcony.

The flames from a massive garden urn of wax are reflected in the glass door.

OPPOSITE: Wherefore art thou. . . ?

There are a number of ways to approach celebrating this season with candles. Classic settings of fall colors using leaves, flowers, and candles are a very simple and beautiful way to enjoy this time of year. Varieties of candle colors, textures, and shapes are another way of highlighting the traditional ideals of autumn. I create some of my favorite settings by using traditional elements in unconventional ways. For example, I love to use candles with pumpkins—but without carving haunting grins on a single one. Whatever your preference, fall is a time of imagination and magic. Create a setting that enables you to appreciate autumn's art in the world around you.

OPPOSITE: A bath warmed with golden light and colorful flowers.

ABOVE: We chose salmon candles to blend with the walls and speared sunflowers to the candle-holders. The flowers all came from the garden. Tapers lend elegant height to the table setting.

A celebration that is not necessarily confined to autumn (but how nice when it happens during this time!) represents one of the most important uses of candles. Birthday celebrations would not be the same without candles on the cake. Don't worry—the number of candles may vary, as do the number of ways to make your wishes come true. A romantic table with tall salmon tapers sprouting from sunflowers atop silver candlesticks, a birthday cake ready for anyone's wishes, or a candle-laden bath with flowers aglow: a special day can become even more so.

Doesn't this photograph capture everyone's first memory of candles?

Bittersweet scented candles in the window beckoning us inside echo the fragrance of autumn leaves burning. Enjoy the last dinner outdoors on the terrace surrounded by flickering candles and chenille throws. Set an individual votive at each place setting and tie the napkin with a ribbon to mimic the motion of the candle flame. Or, gather a handful of leaves, sweet gum balls, and pinecones, and add a tall autumn-fragranced candle to celebrate the change of seasons. Bring indoor elements out into the fresh air. Take a tablecloth adorned with dancing leaves, and team it with transfer ware, lusterware, and other mismatched pieces. Add graduated hurricanes, serve the bounty of the season, and savor the color of the leaves surrounding you.

FROM THE TERRACE

Enjoy the stillness outside by once again bringing the indoors out. A tablecloth of dancing leaves, an array of tableware, the warmth of the terrace.

PUT SOME POISON IN IT

We loved the poison green of the streaked goblets so much that we streaked the tapers with florist spray and anchored them in the bois d'arc apples, surrounding them with purple statice.

WICK-ED

Okay—you recognize the holiday. Everything here plays off the colors in the Warhol lithograph. Rather than pumpkins, we used vintage glass and mixed column candles. Purple is regal and we filled an ice bucket with our favorite bois d'arcs and even used them, cored out, to hold the tapers. Dramatic, as well as romantic, Margaret Hamilton's character never had it so hot.

Halloween provides an ideal opportunity to use one's imagination. There are no barriers to this holiday. Adults often delight in this fall festival as much as, if not more than, children. Bales of hay, stalks of corn, and scary jack-o'-lanterns seem to linger around most homes. Personally, I prefer to be a little less traditional in my approach. Come October, I call *The Witch* into the dining room. Rather than pumpkins, I bring out vintage glass and mixed column candles. The orange is a nice foil for the witch's complexion, which is reinforced with chartreuse tapers. Everything plays off the colors in the print. The normally prim and proper African violet seems a bit of purple poison in this territory. Dramatic, but not too scary, Margaret Hamilton's character provides quite a spectacle to the children of all ages who pass by my windows.

⤠   While I decided to use less traditional components with art as my focus for Halloween, pumpkins are a great part of the fall harvest and are one of my favorite things to include. As I was selecting pumpkins, the grower gave me the names and explained the types that he had for sale. When he pointed out the "Cinderella" variety I knew instantly that carving a face would not be the most effective use of it. To transform this pumpkin I applied gold leaf with a paintbrush to highlight its shape. The stem was replaced with a pewter crown, and a gold-leaf column cap from a craft store became the throne. I then inserted wire prongs to hold gold-leaf votive cups. Masses of cerise dahlias and trailing potato vine pay tribute to this regal pumpkin.

OPPOSITE: A mini pumpkin wears an Italianate filigree jeweled crown and rests comfortably on gold-leafed potato leaves.

RIGHT: No bales of hay here. We avoided shocks of wheat and false harvest scenes and gave our pumpkin regal stature. Fittingly, this variety is called "Cinderella."

Imagining Cinderella's candlelit carriage—rather than headless horsemen—is another way to incorporate pumpkins into the holiday. Instead of traditional ghoulish themes, conjure up magical fantasy. A new white variety of pumpkins called "Ghost" were my inspiration to continue Cinderella's journey. Elevating the mighty pumpkin to a more enchanted position, I placed it on a silver wine bucket and decorated it with votive candles and fairy dust. We cut out the carriage door and window, created a coat of arms, and gold-leafed it. We even touched each flaw on the pumpkin with paint and lined the pumpkin opening with gold. We replaced the stem with a silver wine stopper and placed a candle in a votive inside. The carriage frame is an antique English sterling potato warmer, the wheels are silver wine coasters, the spokes are mini pumpkins resting on more miniatures. A Victorian silver meat fork serves as the carriage tongue. The silver pattern is called "Love Disarmed." We surrounded Cinderella with column candles, silver votives, and antique bud vases and placed it all on a shimmering mirror. Who wouldn't want to arrive at the ball in such style? Your entire room will gather around this pumpkin although it's far, far removed from a jack-o'-lantern's lopsided grin. This fairy-tale approach is perfect for children, but adults will be taken with its magic as well.

MOONLIGHT AND IVORY

What colors do you associ-
ate with Halloween? That's
what we thought, too, until
we availed ourselves of the
new white variety of pumpkin called "Ghost." We nested
it in boxwood, ivy, and
stephanotis atop a sterling
wine cooler, and paired it
with white column votives
and silver serving pieces on
our table. Unexpected and
dramatic, our table still
evokes a childlike simplicity.

BELOW: Our smaller pumpkin,
chosen for contrasting texture, has a lamp finial as a
sort of feather in its cap.

Who wouldn't want to arrive at the ball in such style? We surrounded Cinderella with column candles, silver votives, and antique bud vases simulating turrets and placed it all on a shimmering mirror.

Further varying the theme of fright-free Halloween, I decided to construct a Pumpkin Town. Taking inspiration from the mice that sewed Cinderella's dress, I used dollhouse doors and windows to create individual pumpkin cottages. The pumpkins were carved out and lit with candles—their natural long stems made the perfect chimneys. The street is made of weathered whitewashed boards. Sprigs of boxwood sheared into trees and shrubs were placed into small pumpkins. The autumnal landscape was completed with marigolds and ivy leaves. A mini pumpkin on a votive throne with a tiny doll's candelabra provided the final over-the-top element that completed the village.

We gold-leafed the doorframe and flanked it with tiny coach lights. We thought it important to include a surprise inside: We placed a mini pumpkin on a votive "throne" and placed a candelabra on top. This could be the most enchanted evening a mouse ever had!

WON'T YOU TAKE ME TO PUMPKIN TOWN?

The mice had to live somewhere while they sewed Cinderella's dress—here's their block! We assembled it with field pumpkins, dollhouse parts, and fresh foliage. After carving out the pumpkins, we lit them with candles, using their stems as whimsical chimneys. The sheer effect at the windows results from scraping away the pumpkin shell and leaving the membrane as a sort of curtain. The smaller pumpkins serve as pots, holding crape myrtle foliage and marigolds. Tiny terra-cotta pots hold clipped pieces of boxwood.

Pumpkins can hold more than candles. Their magical qualities work well with flowers, too. I cut off the top of one and fastened it with florist's tape so it served as a platform for our votive in a golden terra-cotta pot. I then placed an oasis in the cavity to secure the fall-toned flowers. Surrounded by fallen petals and more votives, the pumpkin rests on a vanity tray. Candles can work as well on the outside as the inside.

Here, the pumpkins hold rich autumn colors
of mums and roses rather than candles.

107

When November rolls around with its invigorating crispness, I take stock of the firewood and check the candle inventory. Those column candles I enjoyed earlier this fall are ready for a wick trimming. As the flame recedes behind a veil of wax they provide a soft glowing effect. Mix these oddly curled columns with new tapers and fresh votive candles for a variation of flames and light. Guests can sense that you are accustomed to creating the perfect settings.

The foyer chest that greets visitors should reflect the autumn tones. Cinnamon-toned candles were selected for the tallest spindle candleholders and warmer, red tones were placed on the table nearest the arrangement, graduating the color depth. The bountiful arrangement in a black urn includes fruit of the season, as well as flowers and candles. The mirror doubles the candlepower, providing depth. The glossy table surface of inlaid wood also reflects the glow. Candles, fruit, and flowers—what better way to create a welcoming feel?

Reflections in a golden eye. The bountiful arrangement includes fruits of the season, as well as flowers, all in a black urn.

We placed a red column on a filigree stand and surrounded it with cranberries. The grapes, persimmon, and pomegranate reinforce the intensity of the color.

Here, allied with greenery,
purple larkspur, and baby
pineapples, we dressed a pillar,
giving it a choker and let it
glow amid the festivity.

Color plays a large part in the excitement of fall. The bold, beautiful fall colors balance spring's delicacy. The artful balance of each season affords a wonderful opportunity to express our own creativity. Use your imagination to create something extraordinary out of anything you enjoy. I chose proteas and pomegranates to compete with persimmons and dahlias for the candlelight. Marble- and stone-finished candles in this palette provided harmony and added warmth to the table. Estate-sale finds of mismatched jewelry give this setting an extra sparkle: Previously burned column candles were wrapped in ribbon and adorned with solitary earrings to ornament the setting. Their stones pick up the light from the candles and supply unexpected glamour to a traditional dinner table. Look at your own world and see how you can make it sparkle.

Our favorite curling shape of a mature candle reposes in its cocoon of ribbon and jeweled badge, all placed in an antique goblet. The drooping tops of the previously burned candles add an organic, natural shape to the tablescape.

The Macy's Thanksgiving Day Parade is over and we are all bracing ourselves for the rush of the holidays. When I was growing up on the farm, the Saturday after Thanksgiving would have been spent on horseback with my father and brothers. We would ride in search of the perfect tree to put in the same spot in the living room—it never changed. When we found the tree on which we could all agree, we would mark it with a bright red bandanna. A couple of weeks later we would return to cut down the tree along with an assortment of evergreen and berry branches, and carry it all home. Mother would be the one to carefully unwrap the ornaments, but decorating the tree was always a family affair. (I am sure, however, that she made many necessary adjustments when we were not present.)

Lights define the tree, and candles extend and sustain that light, spreading it from room to room. Nothing expresses the joy of the season better than masses of glowing lights, no matter their source. Christmas is a perfect time to use both electricity and the primal glow of candles.

The boxes with the tree ornaments also contained the Christmas candles, which were hand-carved and painted and truly special. These symbols of the season had pre-determined destinations in the house too. The traditions we honor at special times of the year are a large part of who we are, and candles are used in most of these traditions. The simplicity of candlelight makes a grand statement. Columns of candles set the season ablaze. Tiny votives shimmer in unexpected corners. The warmth, suggestive of less complicated times, fills the room, transforming the ordinary into the extraordinary.

A votive, simple blossom, and two cherries with stems
echo the larger piece, playing up its natural beauty.
Smaller re-creations like this evoke a pleasing symmetry.

A wax cherub balances a cherry in his hand.

Candlelight provides instant atmosphere for the season's celebrations. Winter is a time of reflection and celebration with family and friends. As I plan my holiday entertaining, I literally go all through the house to ensure that there is an ambience from the front door to the back. I determine the most effective placement of candles to set the desired mood. At my house everyone enters through the front door. My intention is to greet all the guests and establish the tone for the occasion. I make the first impression a lasting one by creating a candlelight path to the front door. I always use scented candles, which sets the mood even before the evening begins. Outside you can use

stronger evergreen or spice-perfumed candles to provide a hint of the festivities within. The fragrances of clove, cinnamon, vanilla, and holiday spices magically conjure up childhood memories. You don't have to bake a loaf of bread or make a cake: We have the ability to re-create these memories through fragrant candles. This season's gatherings are spiced by our imagination.

After lighting the candles, I turn off all the electrical lights. This allows me to observe the pools of candlelight and adjust the placement to their best advantage. When I turn the lights back on, I dim them. This gives guests a sense of harmony as they wander about the house. In the entrance hall an antique iron-and-marble table filled with candles and flowers greets the guests. When massing groups of candles it works best to remain within a color family. This directs attention to the play of light and the effect it has on the flowers and surrounding accessories. As I focus on the dinner table I uncover a collection of cherub candles that seem delighted to be unboxed. Taking a simple bowl on a stand swathed in iridescent ribbon, I fill it with a column candle, alstroemeria, roses, and luscious cherries. Clustering the cherubs with these simple elements provides an unexpected but warm and cheerful setting for a winter's evening.

Ward off the winter chill. We took a simple
bowl on a stand swathed in iridescent ribbon,
filled it with a column candle, alstroemeria,
roses, and luscious cherries. Simple elements,
yet so unexpected on a cold evening.

121

INSIDE OUT

OPPOSITE: A trail of votive candles leads
the guests with light and fragrance to the
entrance of my home. Lanterns cast flickering shadows at eye level, reminding us of a
time gone by. There is an anticipation of
evening as friends are drawn into the foyer.

Maintaining a mix of candle heights, I filled
the refractory table with new and old column and votive candles. The four columns
in the foreground are snug in an antique
wooden sugar mold. The cymbidium orchid
and the Mark Stock pastel provide depth
and movement.

Christmas at my friend's house on Jackson Street was, well, delicious. We used a classic Della Robbia theme. The colors danced around reds, greens, and gold and yet seemed fresh and new. Amethyst glass and almost-black grapes and berries pushed the colors forward. In this setting the candles are as important for their tonal quality as they are for producing the glow that seems to extend the light from the Christmas tree. The candles on the table echo the fruits in forms and colors.

The dolphin urn serves beautifully as a container for pillars of graduated height, votives, fruit, and greenery. The glossy grapes mirror the light reflected in the arching dolphins.

OPPOSITE: A flat newel post is a perfect place for a multiwick column surrounded by greenery and kumquats on a silver tray. (Alert any guests who might be tempted to slide down the banister Christmas morning!)

LEFT: Playing on the traditional reds and greens of the season.

OPPOSITE: A pair of cobalt urns, once part of a vanity set, finds new life as votive holders

Little touches of candlelight around the house can provide an element of surprise and a feeling of discovery. It also affords an opportunity to use your favorite things in a new way. A candle shimmering in a blue bowl beneath flowers on a dresser adds romance to the moment. On a side table we play a trick on the red-and-green holiday theme with strawberries surrounding a cranberry column candle atop a classic pedestal with a bowl of Granny Smith apples nearby. An antique birdbath-style salt dish becomes the perfect votive holder on a stamped Moroccan leather table. A pair of cobalt urns finds new life as votive holders. Your guests will wonder why they did not think to do that!

A cranberry candle, mimicking the color of the stamped Moroccan leather-clad table, sits in an antique birdbath-style salt dish.

A candle shimmers in a blue bowl beneath flowers on a dresser.

I was hosting a dinner party on Christmas Eve. Because the guests had all been to my home many times before, I wanted to create a different and glamorous setting lit by candles and the Christmas tree. The living room has a fireplace and a beautiful view of the garden, so I transformed it into a dining space. Then I decided to have a pair of Christmas trees rather than one. The change may sound odd, but why not try something different that renews the spirit of the holidays? Flanking the fireplace, the trees created a dramatic setting.

129

If your room (and your budget) can stand it, why not trim two Christmas trees? Try to find two that are as close in size to each other as possible and decorate them similarly.

One of my dear friends loaned me Warhol's *Santa* for the occasion. A pair of Florentine gold-leaf candelabra fragments worked with the red candles on the dining table and drew the eye to the fireplace, which was filled with more of the cinnamon-scented candles. A boxwood wreath on the French door was encased in a gold frame, which reflected the candlelight and seemed suspended in air. The living room was now a cozy dining area, and the garden's lights and candles gave the room an extended view of holiday glitter.

OPPOSITE: To accompany
our red candles, we used a
spare arrangement of Monet
poinsettias, parrot tulips,
and magnolia foliage in a
column capital.

Candles provided a festive element in bright colors
for my Christmas dinner party, but their romantic qualities are also obvious. Candlelight is magical. Its powers
can enchant a large dinner party, or make intimate an
evening for two. Candles can also serve to prepare us for
a special evening. Forgotten everyday areas, such as a
dressing table, are perfect for candles. Tapers, columns,
and votives augment the warm lamplight. The glimmer
of candles reflected in the crystal perfume bottles creates
an entrancing spell.

We hung a boxwood wreath on the French
doors and found a gold frame to encase
it. The frame, reflecting the candlelight,
seems suspended in air.

Sometimes we collect disparate pieces, never anticipating that once placed together they will take on new meaning. The wrought-iron fragment in back is from a New Orleans balcony, the black candlesticks are old marble from an estate sale, the iron sconce in the center is from Chicago. An arrangement of proteas and pomegranates provides the structure that pulls it all together.

OPPOSITE: The votive holder is also a fragment, once part of a fixture. Placed in front of the sconce, propped on a pomegranate, it becomes part of a larger entity.

Sometimes there is nothing more satisfying than paring
down. All we have here are blown-glass candle holders with
colored bottoms, an Italian crystal bowl with roses, and a
mirror to reflect and multiply the cool organic shapes.

Bruce and Sally invited friends to celebrate New Year's Eve with a candlelit dinner. Their favorite flowers were dusted with sugar and glitter so that they shimmered in the soft light of the candles. Beautiful collections of silver, china, and treasured heirlooms were incorporated to make the table even more elegant.

The candle holder, a snow-ball votive, brings light down from the chandelier to the tabletop.

LEFT: Ice-blue ivy trailing down the candelabra echoes the swirl in the wax tapers.

OPPOSITE: Fire and Ice— the uniformity of the spiral tapers echoes the chandelier above this richly set holiday table. The use of white in a deeply toned room magnifies the intensity of the light. The silver reflects the light even further.

We created our "ice" on the flowers by dipping them in egg white, sugar, and diamond dust. Predominantly white flowers reinforce the power of white tapers, and the "ice" suspends the flowers in time, a subversive touch for a New Year's dinner. We stuck in a bunch of violets to anchor the otherwise all-white arrangement.

ABOVE: A silver champagne goblet contains a mauve column surrounded with roses. The votive in the green glass container seems to meld into its surroundings, despite its solitary flame.

OPPOSITE: Most of the tablescapes we have featured in our book are either dining or entry. The intimate scene here is a dressing table. Tapers, columns, and votives augment the warm lamplight. The glimmer of candles reflected in the many bottles and vials creates an entrancing magic.

ABOVE: One of our favorite shots, this photograph
captures the movement of time, the gentle interplay
of fire and air on the candle itself.

OPPOSITE: The tapers on the ledge above the bed
create the illusion of height, yet the candles burning
on the tray and the two glasses and wine bucket
underscore the intimacy of the setting.

Candlelight is a wonderful way to distract attention from a piece's flaws and to focus instead on its mood. The three-dollar garage sale centerpiece I found is a good example. Chipped and discolored, this heart-shaped centerpiece is made flawless with pink sweetheart roses and simple votives.

A HEARTFELT SALUTE

We found this heart-shaped ring and cupids at a yard sale. We filled it with pink spray roses, ivy, and jasmine, and an occasional votive. Once again, the romance is apparent even with the limited use of materials. At left, Cupid stands sentry over the flames and flowers.

Even with today's sophisticated lighting, we can't replace the magical romantic qualities that candles offer. When used imaginatively, they can set a tone for a special occasion or make an ordinary day more memorable. The extent of what can be accomplished is limited only by our creativity. Indoors or out, daytime or evening, holiday or everyday, candles are an easy, affordable way to improve our surroundings. They can light our path, greet our guests, and provide elegant atmosphere for entertaining. During my career in developing new candles, containers, and fragrances, I have witnessed them constantly evolve to accommodate every situation and personality. Candles are now available in almost limitless styles, colors, and fragrances, making it easier to celebrate your life by candlelight.

Informal settings are also made
romantic with candlelight. Patrick's
casual collection of Asian imports
and sleek modern furniture are
softened by a variety candle styles.

Acknowledgments

HOMES, GARDENS, AND ACCESSORIES: Michael Banic; Bill Barranger; Annacha Briggs; Tim Carter and Robert Broughton; Phil Cato; Amy Colclasure; Todd Estes; John Golden; Thom Hall; Keith James; Park Lanford; Stephen Lanford; Buddy McConnell; Mary Murray; Patrick Phillips; Brett Pitts and Kevin Walsh; Renee and Scott Rittlemeyer; Sally and Bruce Sanderson; Ellen Scruggs; Catherine Smith; Ken Stone; Jon Stone; Adrienne and Brad Taylor; Rus Venable; Holly Vines; Nancy and Bill Wade; Keith Wooten.

BUSINESSES IN LITTLE ROCK ARKANSAS: The Accessory; Arkansas Art Center; The Art of the Party; At Home Arkansas; Bear-Hill Interiors; The City Farmer; Cobblestone & Vine; Dauphine; Hocott's Garden; Marshall-Clements; Massimo; Mertins-Dyke; Nola Studios; Pasha Bass Interiors; Randall Byars Interiors; Southern Wholesale Florist; Tipton & Hurst; Wordsworth Books.

OTHER BUSINESSES: Archipelago Botanicals, Los Angeles, California; Blue Moon Gallery, Hot Springs, Arkansas; Couleur Nature, Chula Vista, California; El Deco, Nashville, Tennessee; Esplanade, Friendswood, Texas; Jim Marvin Enterprises, Dixon, Tennessee; Seasons, by Fitz and Floyd, Lewisville, Texas; Trambow Family, Celaya Guanjuato, Mexico; The Villa, Hot Springs, Arkansas; Zodax, Van Nuys, California.

Birthday in the Barrio

Cumpleaños en el Barrio

Story / Cuento
Mayra L. Dole

Illustrations / Ilustraciones
Tonel

Children's Book Press / Editorial Libros para Niños
San Francisco, California

Rosario's sister Lazarita is mad at her dad. **"Pipo, I want my *quinces* in a** BIG **Miami dance hall!"** she gripes.

Her father scratches his bushy mustache. "*Mi niña*, we have no money for a fancy party, not even for your fifteenth birthday. You know I lost my job."

Lazarita cries, "But Pipo, I want to step out of a swan boat. I want a live band, dancers, and a banquet."

"You can have a house party and I'll come with my congas!" I suggest.

Lazarita **STORMS** into her room. Today she is like a big plate of *frijoles negros*, the black beans that give you a bellyache if you eat too many!

Lazarita, la hermana de Rosario, está furiosa con su papá y protesta: —**¡Pipo, quiero celebrar mis quinces en un salón de baile bien GRANDE!**

Su padre rasca su espeso bigote. —Mi niña, no tenemos dinero para una fiesta como ésa, ni siquiera porque son tus quinces. Ya sabes que estoy sin trabajo.

Lazarita lloriquea: —Pero Pipo, yo quiero bajar de un bote en forma de cisne, y quiero una orquesta, muchas parejas y un buffet.

—Mejor sería una fiestecita en casa. ¡Puedo tocar la tumbadora! —le sugiero.

Lazarita se va *furiosísima* a su cuarto. Hoy está más pesada que un enorme plato de **frijoles negros**, ¡de esos que te dan tremendo dolor de estómago si comes más de la cuenta!

3

Rosario and I are sitting waaaaaay up in a mango tree. I pick a mango and peel it. "Such a fuss about turning fifteen. All I want for my birthday are *tumbadora* drums! But Lazarita'll be mad if she doesn't have a *quinces* like the other girls."

Rosario agrees. "Chavi, Lazarita's usually so understanding about Pipo's job. She's always baby-sitting after school to help pay the bills."

I take a big juicy mango bite. "HEY! Maybe Dalili's *mima* can help us throw Lazarita a *quinces* party! She's always organizing fancy events."

"**Bárbaro!**" Rosario slaps me a messy-mango high five.

Rosario y yo estamos sentadas en lo alto de la mata de mangos. Agarro uno y lo pelo. —¡Tanto cuento con los quinces! Yo me conformo con una tumbadora el día de mi cumpleaños, pero Lazarita se va a enojar si no se los celebran como a las demás.

Rosario está de acuerdo: —Chavi, Lazarita se ha portado muy bien desde que Pipo perdió el empleo... y hasta trabaja de niñera después de clases para ayudarlo.

Doy una gran mordida a mi mango. —OYE, quizás la mima de Dalili nos pueda ayudar. Ella organiza fiestas muy elegantes.

—¡**Bárbaro!** —dice Rosario, dándome una fuerte palmada en mi mano, con su mano embarrada de mango.

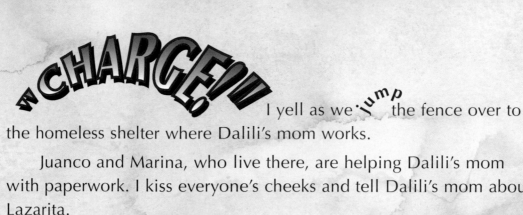

"**CHARGE!**" I yell as we jump the fence over to the homeless shelter where Dalili's mom works.

Juanco and Marina, who live there, are helping Dalili's mom with paperwork. I kiss everyone's cheeks and tell Dalili's mom about Lazarita.

"I'd love to do something special in honor of Lazarita's *quinces*, but Chavi, I'm too busy. We are having trouble raising money to keep the shelter open."

I have an idea. "How about if we have a *quinces* party that also raises money for the shelter?"

Dalili's mom's face sparkles. "***Niña, síííí!*** Okay, here's what you two *maripositas* must do to help organize the event . . ."

—¿AL ATAQUE!

—grito cuando saltamos la cerca del albergue de desamparados donde trabaja la mamá de Dalili.

Juanco y Marina, que viven allí, están ayudando en la oficina. Les doy besitos a todos y les hago el cuento de los quinces.

—Me encantaría poder hacer algo especial para los quinces de Lazarita, Chavi, pero estoy muy ocupada. Se nos está haciendo difícil recaudar fondos para el albergue.

De pronto se me ocurre una idea. —¿Qué les parece si celebramos los quinces y a la vez recaudamos dinero para el albergue?

A la mamá de Dalili se le iluminan los ojos.
—*¡Niña, síííí!* Vamos a ver... Miren, maripositas, lo que tienen que hacer ustedes para organizar la fiesta es lo siguiente...

"¡Uno, dos, tres! Go!"

We swoosh onto Sarita's front porch. Her skinny-as-a-palm-tree
father greets us with kisses. ☞ Smack! ☜

I explain, "We're planning the BIGGEST party in the world
for Lazarita's *quinces*, but we have no food." I put on my saddest face.
"We need your help or the guests will starve."

He grumbles, "*Ay, niña,* I can't feed all those people."
"Well, that's okay. We'll ask Rauli's father! He makes the best
puerco asado in all Miami!"

"Mine is a million times better than his!" He kisses all five fingertips
at once. **"I'll make a *puerco asado* with *mojito* to die for."**

—¡Uno, dos, tres, p'alante!

—Así entramos corriendo en el
portal de la casa de Sarita. Su papá, alto y flaco como una palma real, nos
da besitos: ☞ —Muuuá! ¡Muuuá! ☜

Le explico: —Le estamos organizando la fiesta más GRANDE del mundo
a Lazarita, pero no hemos conseguido comida. —Pongo una cara bien triste—.
Necesitamos que nos ayude.

El papá de Sarita se queja: —Ay, niña, no puedo cocinar para tanta gente.

—Bueno, entonces... Se lo pedimos al papá de Rauli; ¡él cocina el mejor
puerco asado de Miami!

—El mío es un millón de veces mejor. —Se besa las puntas de los dedos—.
Yo les haré un puerco asado con mojito como para chuparse los dedos.

"Last one in is a rotten *guayaba*!" I screech as Rosario and I splash into Rauli's plastic pool.

"*Hola, corazoncitos!*" Rauli's father's **WATERMELON BELLY** wiggles.

"Sarita's father says his *puerco asado* is better than yours!" I trumpet.

Rauli's dad slaps his cheek. "Then Sarita's father is *loco* in the head!"

"Sarita's father is so good," I add, "he's going to cook for Lazarita's *quinces*!"

"And I was not invited to cook? That's preposterous!"

Rosario shakes her ringlets dry. "Then we'll have a *barrio* cooking contest!"

"*Fenómeno!* You'll see," he boasts, **"no one can beat my prize-winning *puerco asado*!"**

10

Rosario y yo nos lanzamos a la piscina de Rauli. —**¡La última en llegar es una guayaba podrida!** —grito.

—Hola, corazoncitos —dice el papá de Rauli. Su **BARRICA DE MELÓN** tiembla.

—¡El papá de Sarita dice que su puerco asado es el mejor! —digo.

El padre de Rauli se da una palmada en el cachete. —Si dijo eso está loco, tocado del queso.

—Es muy buen cocinero —sigo— y va a cocinar para los quinces de Lazarita.

—Y a mí, ¿no me invitaron? ¡Eso es ridículo!

Rosario agita la cabeza para secarse los rizos.

¡Entonces tendremos competencia de cocineros en el barrio! –asegura.

—**Fenómeno!** Van a ver. **¡A mí no hay quien me gane asando puercos!**

—alardea el papá de Rauli.

"On your mark, get set, *fueeraaaa!*" I yell. We race through Chuli's front door.

The walls are filled with paintings of saints. Chuli's grandma Josefina wants to be an artist, but instead she works as a baker.

Chuli's *abuelita* **squishes** us into her **marshmallowy** arms. I ask for her help.

"*Amorcito*, I'd have to make ten towering cakes for an event like that!"

Rosario laughs. "You could make cake sculptures!"

"Besides," I hold the *abuelita's* hand, "it's a **party** to help the homeless shelter."

Her wrinkles soften. "In that case, *mis florecitas,* count me in!"

—¡En sus marcas, listas, *fueeraaaa!*" —grito al entrar a toda velocidad en casa de Chuli.

Las paredes están llenas de cuadros de santos. La abuelita de Chuli, Abuelita Josefina, quiere ser pintora, pero trabaja en una panadería.

Ella nos **aprieta** con sus brazos de **melcocha**. Le pido ayuda.

—¡Ay, amorcito, para una fiesta así tendría que hacer diez pasteles de diez pisos!

Rosario ríe. —¡Los podría hacer como si fueran esculturas de dulce!

—Y además —le tomo la mano a la abuelita,— será una **fiesta** para ayudar a los desamparados del albergue.

Las arrugas se le ablandan. —Pues entonces, mis florecitas, cuenten conmigo.

13

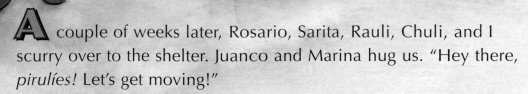

A couple of weeks later, Rosario, Sarita, Rauli, Chuli, and I scurry over to the shelter. Juanco and Marina hug us. "Hey there, *pirulíes!* Let's get moving!"

Kids from the shelter are practicing a line dance to **blasting** music. People make decorations and blow up balloons. We lug fat bags of beans, rice, napkins, and paper plates into the shelter kitchen. We've gotten donations from all the grocery stores in the neighborhood.

Juanco lets us know, "Tomorrow we will set up and decorate Ocean Drive early."

Dalili asks me, **"You got permission to close the street, right, Chavi?"**

UH-OH! Rosario and I look at each other. **"We'll be right back!"**

Un par de semanas después, Rosario, Sarita, Rauli, Chuli y yo llegamos corriendo al albergue. Juanco y Marina nos abrazan: —¡Eh, pirulíes, a trabajar, que para luego es tarde!

Los niños del albergue ya están ensayando una coreografía, con una música que nos deja sordos, mientras los adultos hacen decoraciones e inflan globos. Nosotros llevamos a la cocina las bolsas de frijoles, arroz, servilletas y platos de papel que nos donaron en los mercados y bodeguitas del barrio.

—Mañana bien tempranito empezamos a montar el quiosco en Ocean Drive —dice Juanco.

Dalili me pregunta: **—Chavi ¿pediste el permiso para cerrar la calle, verdad?**

—¡AY, AY, AY! Rosario y yo nos miramos—. **Enseguida regresamos** —decimos, y salimos volando.

I run to Zuli's house, so fast I **BOING** into her *abuelito's* beach ball belly. He works for the city manager. I boom, **"We forgot to ask you to get the special permit to block the street for a *fiesta*!"**

"It's not so easy. Don't you know that permits take months?"

"Then," I insist, **"I will ask the president of the United States!"**

His moustache flips up and down as he cracks up laughing. "Not even the president can help you. You could ask the mayor but, at this point, he can't help either!"

Entramos en casa de Zuli tan rápido que —¡BOING!— choco contra la barriga de su abuelito, quien trabaja en el ayuntamiento. Le digo: —**¡Se nos olvidó pedirle que nos consiguiera un permiso para cerrar la calle para una fiesta!**

—Eso no es tan fácil. Los permisos demoran meses —dice el abuelito.

—Pues entonces —insisto— **¡se lo pediré al mismísimo presidente de los Estados Unidos!**

El abuelo también ríe, y su bigote sube y baja. —¡Ni el presidente las podría ayudar! ¡Vayan a ver al alcalde, pero, a estas alturas, dudo que él pueda hacer algo!

City Hall is as **wide** as the beach and as **tall** as the clouds. We storm in, followed by Juanco and Marina. We find the mayor in the hallway with his two daughters.

"Mr. Mayor!" I blurt out everything about the party and the shelter to him; I tell him we *absolutely* have to have a permit.

"Sorry, girls," the mayor shakes his head. "Zuli's grandfather is right. There's nothing I can do on such short notice."

One daughter bursts in, "*Papi*, I just had my *quinces*. Every girl should have a *quinces*."

"*Please, pleeeease*," we beg. "We need someone to block the street. This party will really help the shelter."

"I'm so very sorry," the mayor sighs. **"It can't be done."**

El ayuntamiento es **ancho** como la playa y tan **alto** que casi llega a las nubes. Entramos alborotadas. En el pasillo están el alcalde y sus dos hijas.

   —¡Señor alcalde, por favor! —grito. Me acerco, y le cuento los detalles de la fiesta y la recaudación, insistiendo en cómo necesitamos el permiso.

   —El abuelito de Zuli tenía razón —responde el alcalde—. No puedo hacer nada en tan poco tiempo.

   Una de las hijas dice: —Papá, yo acabo de celebrar mis quinces. A todas las niñas se les deben celebrar los quinces.

   —¡Por favor! ¡Por favooooor! —le rogamos—. Necesitamos el permiso. Esta fiesta va a ayudar a mantener el albergue.

   —Lo siento. **No puedo hacer nada** —dice el alcalde, apenado.

Today is Lazarita's birthday. We've decided that, since we can't have a party, we will buy her gifts to cheer her up.

We **dash** by the fruit store, **zip** past the hardware store, **turn** the corner by the beauty shop, and get to the Dollar Store. Then, we head to Rosario's house with the cool stuff we've chosen.

I hand Lazarita a friendship bracelet. "How beautiful, Chavi." Lazarita kisses my cheek.

Rosario hands her a plastic tiara with shiny stones. Lazarita gives her a big hug.

But in spite of our little gifts, I feel very bad that we couldn't give Lazarita the best party in the whole wide world.

Hoy es el cumpleaños de Lazarita. Decidimos que, como no habrá fiesta, vamos a animarla comprándole regalitos.

Salimos **disparadas** a la frutería y la quincalla, y luego **doblamos** por la esquina de la peluquería, entramos en la Tienda del Dólar y después volvemos a casa de Rosario con todas las cositas bellas que escogimos.

Le doy una linda pulsera de amistad a Lazarita. —¡Qué preciosa, Chavi! —Lazarita me da un besito en el cachete.

Rosario le regala una tiara plástica con brillantes, y Lazarita le da un abrazo enorme.

Pero, a pesar de los regalitos, me siento muy triste porque no pudimos celebrarle la mejor fiesta del mundo a Lazarita.

It's nighttime. Lazarita comes out wearing the white dress her mother made from her very own wedding gown.

Lazarita's eyes are like two **chocolate** almonds, but sad. She hugs her mother. I think she's stored her *quinces* dreams away in a little secret place in her heart.

Her father gives her a wooden rosary. "This was given to your grandmother on her *quinces*."

Tears sprinkle her face. "I'll treasure it forever. **You're the best father any girl could have.**"

In the middle of all the hugging, the phone rings. "It's Chuli's *abuelita*," I tell everybody. "She wants us to stop by where she's working on Ocean Drive, to pick up a cake for Lazarita's birthday."

22

Es de noche. Lazarita se ha puesto el traje blanco que su mamá le hizo con retazos de su vestido de boda.

Lazarita tiene los ojos como dos almendras de **chocolate**, pero dos almendras tristes. Abraza a su mamá. Parece que ha escondido las ilusiones de los quinces en un rinconcito secreto de su corazón.

Su padre le regala un rosario de madera. —Se lo regalaron a tu abuelita en sus quinces.

Lazarita llora. —Pipo, lo guardaré para siempre. **Eres el mejor padre del mundo** —dice.

Y en medio de tantos abrazos, regalos y lágrimas, suena el teléfono. —Es la abuelita de Chuli —anuncio—. Quiere que pasemos por su trabajo en Ocean Drive a recoger un pastel para Lazarita.

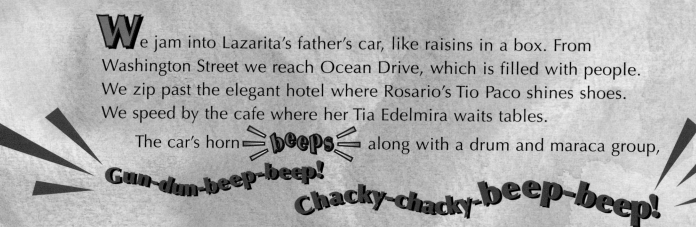

We jam into Lazarita's father's car, like raisins in a box. From Washington Street we reach Ocean Drive, which is filled with people. We zip past the elegant hotel where Rosario's Tio Paco shines shoes. We speed by the cafe where her Tia Edelmira waits tables.

The car's horn **beeps** along with a drum and maraca group,

Gun-dun-beep-beep!

Chacky-chacky-beep-beep!

People bounce up and down and wiggle their hips. ***"Azúcar!"*** They shout as they shake their booties to the rhythm. Something's going on!

"A block party!" Lazarita lights up, surprised like the rest of us.

24

Nos metemos en el carro del papá de Lazarita como pasitas en caja. Llegamos a la calle Washington y de ahí seguimos a Ocean Drive, que está llena de gente. Pasamos frente al restaurante elegantísimo donde limpia zapatos el tío de Rosario, y luego por el café donde su tía Edelmira trabaja de camarera.

Sonamos el claxon al pasar junto a un grupo de personas que tocan tambores y maracas.

¡Gun-dún, bip-bip!   **¡Chaqui-chaqui, bip-bip!**

La gente sube y baja en la calle, meneando las caderas. —¡**Azúcar!** —gritan, siguiendo el ritmo de la música. ¡Algo grande está pasando!

—**¡Una fiesta en plena calle!** —grita Lazarita, tan sorprendida como todos nosotros.

25

What's going on? Chuli's *abuelita* takes us past a long line of colorful food carts filled with *paellas, puercos asados,* and fried *platanitos maduros,* then leads Lazarita to a HUGE cake.

Sarita's father meets us and surprises us even more when he says, "It's a 'Help the Shelter' party! I've made some of my *puerco asado!*"

Rauli's father snorts, **"It's not as good as mine!** You'll see when they award the prize at the cook-off!" Rosario winks at me and whispers, "I bet it will end up in a tie!"

"It looks like an awful lot of people helped, too," I say happily.

Long lines of people pile up for the food. Lazarita jumps in to help Juanco and Marina serve everyone. **"I can't think of a better way to celebrate my quinces!"** she says with delight.

¿**Qué ocurre aquí?** La abuelita de Chuli nos guía por una fila de carritos de comida, repletos de paellas, puercos asados y platanitos maduros fritos, y lleva a Lazarita ante un pastel GIGANTESCO.

El papá de Sarita nos sorprende también: —¡Es una fiesta para ayudar el albergue! ¡Y aquí tienen mi famosísimo puerco asado!

Pero el papá de Rauli refunfuña: —**¡Famosísimo? ¡Vamos a ver quién es el mejor!**

Rosario me guiña un ojo y dice: —Esto va a terminar en empate.

—¡Cuántos han ayudado a hacer esta fiesta! —exclamo con alegría.

Los invitados forman unas colas larguísimas para comer. Lazarita ayuda a Juanco y a Marina a servir, y dice; feliz —**¡Éste es el mejor modo de celebrar mis quinces!**

The mayor takes the microphone. "Ladies and gentlemen, Chavi and Rosario originally planned this party in honor of Lazarita's *quinces*. We grown-ups just took care of some of the little details. **But the girls planned more than just a party—they've brought our entire community together to help our homeless friends!** We congratulate them! So now, enjoy the party, everyone! And don't forget the jars at each table for your donations to the shelter!"

Lazarita is too moved to speak. But Rosario and I throw our fists in the air. **"We did it! We did it!"** The crowd roars!

A slow bolero begins to play, and Lazarita and her father dance along Ocean Drive like two leaves floating on a fresh breeze.

28

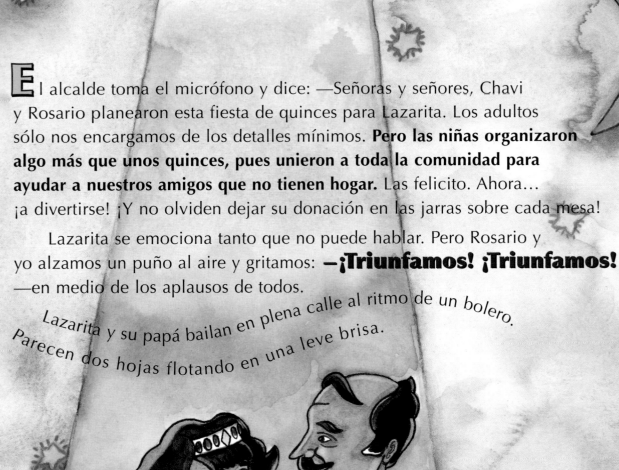

El alcalde toma el micrófono y dice: —Señoras y señores, Chavi y Rosario planearon esta fiesta de quinces para Lazarita. Los adultos sólo nos encargamos de los detalles mínimos. **Pero las niñas organizaron algo más que unos quinces, pues unieron a toda la comunidad para ayudar a nuestros amigos que no tienen hogar.** Las felicito. Ahora… ¡a divertirse! ¡Y no olviden dejar su donación en las jarras sobre cada mesa!

Lazarita se emociona tanto que no puede hablar. Pero Rosario y yo alzamos un puño al aire y gritamos: —**¡Triunfamos! ¡Triunfamos!** —en medio de los aplausos de todos.

Lazarita y su papá bailan en plena calle al ritmo de un bolero. Parecen dos hojas flotando en una leve brisa.

Lazarita hugs Rosario and me *reeeeally* hard. Juanco and Marina tell Rosario's father, "We know it's hard to not be able to give your family what they want. Luckily, you are blessed with caring family and friends."

I see Rosario crying for the first time ever. I whisper into her ear, "Don't worry. We'll find your father a good job."

"That's so hard," she says, drying her tears.

I put my forehead against hers. "If we did this," I tell her, with all my heart,

"we can do anything!"

Lazarita nos abraza *bieeeen* fuerte a Rosario y a mí. Juanco y Marina le dicen al padre de Rosario: —Sabemos lo difícil que es no poder darle a su familia todo lo que se necesita. Pero la mayor bendición que tiene ahora es esta familia y las amistades que los quieren.

Por primera vez en la vida veo llorar a Rosario. Le digo al oído: —No te preocupes. Vamos a conseguirle un buen trabajo a tu papá.

—Eso es bastante difícil —contesta, secándose las lágrimas.

Junto mi frente con la de ella, y le digo de todo corazón: —Si logramos organizar esta fiesta,

¡podremos hacer cualquier cosa!

Mayra L. Dole was born in Marianao, Cuba—the pearl of the Antilles—and raised in Hialeah Florida, a Cuban *barrio,* minutes from Miami. Much like the family in *Birthday in the Barrio,* Mayra's family could not afford a traditional *quinces* party, and, since dancing was Mayra's life, she organized a street dance party instead. A professional dancer in her teens, she also worked as a drummer, and a landscape designer. She describes herself today as a *"barrio* book writer with a beat," and her first book for Children's Book Press, *Drum, Chavi, Drum! / ¡Toca, Chavi, Toca!* is quickly becoming a classic in Latino children's literature.

This story is dedicated to / *Les dedico este cuento a* Mami, Damarys, Mike, Teri, Coky, Paul, Beba, Buffalo, Brian, Rick, Silvia, Salome, Santa, Alina, Tery, Adam, Dr. Daniel Berger, Dr. Robert Cava, Marge Lilly, James Lilly, Penny, Maqui, Syl, Mario, Hortensia, Jason, and Madeline.

My thoughts also go to Papi and Nina (may they rest in peace). / *Pensando siempre en Papi y Nina (que en paz descansen.)*
— **Mayra L. Dole**

Tonel is a visual artist and art critic. He was born in Havana, Cuba, where he designed posters and published illustrations in magazines and newspapers. His work has been exhibited in North and South America, the Caribbean, and Europe. He received a Rockefeller Foundation Fellowship in the Humanities (1997–1998) and a John S. Guggenheim Foundation Fellowship for painting and installation art (1995). In 2003, critics and readers delighted in his lively illustrations for Children's Book Press' acclaimed Cuban-American offering, *Drum, Chavi, Drum! / ¡Toca, Chavi, Toca!*

To my great-grandmother Josefa, to my grandmothers Carolina and Toto, to my grandfather Antonio.

A mi bisabuela Josefa, a mis abuelas Carolina y Toto, a mi abuelo Antonio.
— **Tonel**

Story copyright © 2004 by Mayra L. Dole
Illustrations copyright © 2004 by Tonel

Editors: Ina Cumpiano, Dana Goldberg
Design and production: Carl Angel

Our thanks to Rosalyn Sheff, Diego Vega, and to the staff of CBP.

Library of Congress Cataloging-in-Publication Data

Dole, Mayra L.
Birthday in the barrio / story by Mayra L. Dole; illustrations by Tonel = Cumpleaños en el barrio / cuento de Mayra L. Dole; ilustraciones de Tonel.
    p. cm.
    Summary: When Lazarita's unemployed father cannot afford a party for her "quinces," the birthday celebration that marks a fifteen-year-old girl's entrance into womanhood, her friends in her Miami Cuban-American community enlist the mayor's help to plan a surprise block party.
    ISBN 0-89239-194-4
    [1. Quinceañera (Social custom)—Fiction. 2. Birthdays—Fiction. 3. Parties—Fiction. 4. Friendship—Fiction. 5. Cuban Americans—Fiction. 6. Miami (Fla.)—Fiction. 7. Spanish language materials—Bilingual.] I. Title: Cumpleaños en el barrio. II. Tonel, ill. III. Title.
    PZ73.D6553 2004
    [Fic]—dc22

                                     2004041305

10 9 8 7 6 5 4 3 2 1
Printed in Hong Kong through Marwin Productions.
Distributed to the book trade by Publishers Group West.
Quantity discounts available through the publisher for educational and nonprofit use.

Children's Book Press is a nonprofit publisher of multicultural literature for children. Write us for a complimentary catalog: 2211 Mission Street, San Francisco, CA 94110; (415) 821-3080. Visit our website at www.childrensbookpress.org. A teacher's guide will be available for this book at this website.